W9-CFX-981

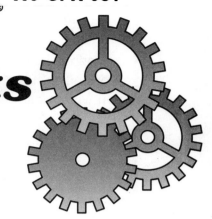

From Your Friends at _The Mailbox_®

Language Arts
MIND BUILDERS
Grade 3

Welcome to _Language Arts Mind Builders_! This must-have resource is sure to reinforce language arts skills while developing critical-thinking skills. Packed with curriculum-based problems and puzzles covering a variety of language arts topics, this resource provides students with a school year's worth of mind-building opportunities.

Project Manager:
Njeri Jones Legrand

Writer:
Laura Wagner

Art Coordinator:
Pam Crane

Artist:
Rebecca Saunders

Cover Artists:
Nick Greenwood, Clevell Harris, Kimberly Richard

www.themailbox.com

Manufactured in the United States
10 9 8 7 6 5 4 3 2 1

INCLUDED IN THIS BOOK

Each activity page features five mind-building language arts problems plus a more difficult bonus builder problem to boost students' critical-thinking skills. Inside you will find an assortment of problems designed to reinforce the language arts skills that you teach. Featured topics and skills include the following:

- word skills
- writing
- reading
- proofreading
- grammar and usage

HOW TO USE THIS BOOK

Use the activity pages in this book in a variety of ways to supplement your language arts curriculum.

 For independent practice, duplicate the activity pages for students to use as morning work, problems of the day, free-time activities, or daily homework practice.

 For partner or small-group practice, duplicate the desired activity pages for each pair or group. Have students discuss possible answers for the problems.

 For whole-group practice, make transparencies of the activity pages.

 For a learning center activity, duplicate, laminate, and cut apart the activity pages. Group the resulting cards by topic and place specific skill cards at a center. Or, for a mixed review, place a variety of skill cards at a center.

 For assessing students' understanding of language arts concepts, make individual student copies and have each student explain in writing his thought process for answering each problem.

WORD SKILLS

Write the five-letter name for each animal. Then write two words that rhyme with each animal name.

①

GRAMMAR & USAGE

List ten nouns that are related to a kitchen.

②

READING

Which word does not belong? Explain your answer.

clock   ring   watch   calendar

③

WRITING

Write three sentences telling what you can do at a park.

④

PROOFREADING

Correct the six mistakes in these sentences.

soccer is my Favorite sport

Whats your favorite Sport.

⑤

BONUS BUILDER #1

If each consonant in the words shown is worth one point and each vowel is worth two points, which word does not total six points?

time
take
toes
torn

WORD SKILLS

WORD SKILLS

Write five short *i* words that have four letters.

(6)

GRAMMAR & USAGE

List five action verbs that begin with the letter *d*.

(7)

READING

Unscramble the boldfaced word in each sentence so that the sentence will make sense.
A. The teacher **dears** to the students every day.
B. Jon hit the ball with the **tab**.
C. Lisa rides the **sub** to school.

(8)

WRITING

Write five sentences that describe how you felt on the first day of school.

Welcome Back

(9)

PROOFREADING

Circle each letter in the sentence that should be capitalized.

mrs. tomie read to randy and carl on tuesday.

(10)

BONUS BUILDER #2

Use the words below to form a question.

the walk room can baby across the

GRAMMAR & USAGE

WORD SKILLS

Kim, Brian, Lori, Cindy, and James are lined up in ABC order. Label each student.

(11)

GRAMMAR & USAGE

What are plural nouns? Give two examples.

(12)

READING

Read the sentence.

Tony put his bathing suit, sunscreen, and towel in his bag.

Write three places Tony might be going.

(13)

WRITING

Hello!

Write three questions you would ask an eagle if it could talk.

(14)

PROOFREADING

What is the total number of mistakes in these sentences?

Casey run as fast as she could to the finnish line?

she won the Race

(15)

BONUS BUILDER #3

Explain what is wrong with this sentence.

Jade walk to Amy's house after school last Monday.

GRAMMAR & USAGE

WORD SKILLS

Write five short *u* words that have more than four letters.

16

GRAMMAR & USAGE

Write each group of words that makes a sentence.

The orange cat on the couch.
Fran likes tomato soup.
The tree swayed in the breeze.

17

READING

Follow the directions.

Draw a circle.
Draw a square inside the circle.
Write an *X* above the circle.

18

WRITING

Write a paragraph about your favorite place.

19

PROOFREADING

Correct each sentence.

close the door

bugs are Comming in the house

20

BONUS BUILDER #4

Which vowel—*a, e, i, o,* or *u*—fits each word?

h__t   r__n
b__g   s__n

WORD SKILLS

WORD SKILLS

Write six words that begin with the letter *t* in ABC order.

21

GRAMMAR & USAGE

Number each lily pad to show what order the words should be in to form a sentence.

- frog
- pond
- the
- into
- The
- leaped

22

READING

What is the main idea of each list?

popcorn	ant
ticket	beetle
large screen	ladybug
candy	dragonfly

23

WRITING

List three things you could do or say to convince your parents to let you stay up an extra hour each night.

24

PROOFREADING

Circle each misspelled word in the sentence. Then write the correct spelling for each circled word.

Jake wint to play tennis with Luke aftar lunch on Saterday.

25

BONUS BUILDER #5

Complete the web. Then use your ideas to write a paragraph about ice cream.

ice cream

WRITING

WORD SKILLS

Which words would not fit on a dictionary page with the guide words *back* and *bring*?

baby	baker
brown	black
bite	bread
bunk	beast
bone	bush

26

GRAMMAR & USAGE

Which has to be used more times to complete the sentences below—*a* or *an*?

____ acorn fell from the tree and ____ squirrel grabbed it.

____ oriole took ____ apple and ____ peach to its nest.

27

READING

Read each sign. Explain what each sign means.

28

WRITING

Write a description of the outfit you are wearing. Draw a picture to match.

29

PROOFREADING

Add punctuation to the sentence.

Aunt Lily took Chase David and Sandy to the park

30

BONUS BUILDER #6

Draw an *X* over each letter that should not be capitalized.

Sarah's Favorite Movie Is *In The Days Of Dinosaurs.* She Plans To Go See It With Her Aunt Rita Next Week.

PROOFREADING

WORD SKILLS

Think about the sound for each word. Which word does not belong? Give two reasons why.

rough   enough
dough   tough

(31)

GRAMMAR & USAGE

Rearrange the words in each sentence to form a question.

The apple is on the table.
The apple is delicious.

(32)

READING

The stegosaurus walked on four legs. It was about 25 feet in length and had horn-covered spines on its tail. Which dinosaur is probably a stegosaurus?

(33)

WRITING

Write three sentences that you might hear a player say who just won a championship game.

(34)

PROOFREADING

Correct the sentence with the most mistakes.

Callie lives in maine and her aunt lives in florida.

they right letters to each other once a month

(35)

BONUS BUILDER #7

Read the clues. Answer the riddle.

I am sometimes shaped like a box.

You can turn me on and off.

I have different channels.

I make noise, but not pictures.

What am I?

WORD SKILLS

Label each picture. Then circle the words that have an equal number of vowels.

GRAMMAR & USAGE

Use the code to underline each sentence.

Code: Statement =
Command =

It's a chilly day.

Please close the door.

The cold air will come inside.

(37)

(36)

READING

Draw a line to separate the words in each question. Then read each question and write an answer.

Doyoulikeicecreamandcake?

Whatkindoficecreamisyourfavorite?

Whatkindofcakeisyourfavorite?

(38)

WRITING

Fill in the blanks to make the story more interesting.

The _____ elf _____ slid down the _____ rainbow and landed in a _____ pot of gold. After digging into the pot, he also found _____ jewels. What a _____ landing!

(39)

PROOFREADING

List the five mistakes in these sentences.

Jalen read the book to paula Sam, and Tanya.

Them liked the stroy

(40)

BONUS BUILDER #8

Write five reasons why traffic signs are important.

WRITING

WORD SKILLS

When rolled, these dice made the word *click*. List five other words that could have possibly been rolled.

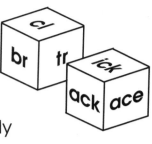

41

GRAMMAR & USAGE

Write the two sentences below as one sentence.

I read a book.

Tina watched a movie.

42

READING

Where would you most likely hear the announcement below? Explain your answer.

Please fasten your seat belts and get ready for takeoff.

43

WRITING

Make a list of ten facts about swimming.

44

PROOFREADING

What are the total number of mistakes in the sentences below?

come down from the tree

I am scary you will fall.

Does you want to get hurt

45

BONUS BUILDER #9

Make a list of 15 long *a* words that have a silent *e* at the end.

WORD SKILLS

WORD SKILLS

Use the key to code each box.

☐ isper   ☐ ade

☐ est   ☐ ame

☐ ase

Key

◩ = sh

◨ = ch

⊞ = wh

(46)

GRAMMAR & USAGE

Write five proper nouns that are related to your city or town.

(47)

READING

Read the answer below. List three possible questions that could have been asked.

Answer: Hot dogs and french fries.

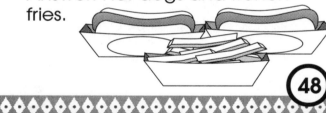

(48)

WRITING

Read the topic sentence below. Then write three details about the topic.

Reading and writing are very important things to learn.

(49)

PROOFREADING

Does the sentence below have more than or less than three mistakes?

it's too hot two sit in the car.

(50)

BONUS BUILDER #10

Read each predicate. What is the subject?

…chases its tail.
…purrs softly.
…has whiskers.

GRAMMAR & USAGE

WORD SKILLS

List five words you could make if you put one letter in each blank.

___ oo ___

(51)

GRAMMAR & USAGE

Circle each noun and draw a box around each verb in the sentences below.

Shelly buys a can of yellow paint.

Shelly paints the kitchen yellow.

(52)

READING

Read the graph. List the students' top two favorite kinds of stories in order, from most to least favorite.

Favorite Kinds of Stories					
Types	Number of Students				
	2	4	6	8	10
Fiction					
Nonfiction					
Fairy Tales					
Tall Tales					
Fables					

(53)

WRITING

Write two sentences to complete the story.

No one answered when Hank rang the bell. "What should I do?" he thought. He had brought a birthday present to give Kent, but it looked like his friend wasn't home.

(54)

PROOFREADING

Add the correct punctuation to the end of each sentence.

Do you want a milk shake

I would like a chocolate milk shake

What a great tasting milk shake

(55)

BONUS BUILDER #11

Find the word that does not fit in each group. Explain your answers.

boot	hoot	toot	foot
treat	heat	great	neat

WORD SKILLS

WORD SKILLS

Which three-letter blend fits each of the word endings below—*scr, spr,* or *str*?

_____ eam   _____ ing

_____ ain   _____ ap

56

GRAMMAR & USAGE

Write the rules for making each noun below a plural noun.

book   leaf   dress   cherry

57

READING

Which word does not belong? Tell how the other three words are related.

football   baseball
soccer   ice skating

58

WRITING

Write an acrostic poem about snow. Begin each line with the letter shown.

S _____

N _____

O _____

W _____

59

PROOFREADING

Correct the sentence.

rebecca found a ear ring on her way home

60

BONUS BUILDER #12

Circle the words that are spelled correctly in the sentence. Correct and list the words that are misspelled.

Push the chare under the kichun tabel.

PROOFREADING

WORD SKILLS

Write five words that would be found on a dictionary page with the guide words *drill* and *drum*.

61

GRAMMAR & USAGE

Make a list of five verbs related to the playground.

62

READING

Read the sentences.

Gina did not eat breakfast. For lunch she ate a salad, a hamburger, french fries, and a cookie. For dinner she ate chicken, rice, and broccoli.

How many different food items did Gina eat?

63

WRITING

Write a description about your best friend's personality.

64

PROOFREADING

Rewrite the letter correctly.

Dear ada I had a wonderful time at you're aunt mary house. Shes a very nice lady. Thank you for a fun day Sincerely Leah

65

BONUS BUILDER #13

Number the events in order from 1 to 4.

☐ Drop a seed in the hole.
☐ Dig a hole in the dirt.
☐ Water the seed and watch it grow.
☐ Cover the seed with dirt.

READING

WORD SKILLS

What three words could you form using the letter cards below?

(66)

GRAMMAR & USAGE

Complete the web.

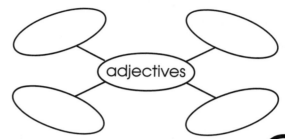

adjectives

(67)

READING

Read the invitation. Write five details about the party.

Top Secret!!
What:
A surprise party for Judy
When:
Saturday, December 30
Where:
123 N. Main St.
RSVP by December 25

(68)

WRITING

Write a letter to your favorite book author asking for an autographed copy of your favorite book.

(69)

PROOFREADING

Add words to fix each sentence.

1. Helped many people.
2. Daniel to the store for.
3. Rushed to hospital.

(70)

BONUS BUILDER #14

Underline the sentence in the paragraph that has the most mistakes.

hurricanes is large storms They brings heavy wind and rain. they can cause a lot of damage People must be careful in hurricanes.

PROOFREADING

WORD SKILLS

Write the silent letter in each word. Then unscramble the letters to create a word that begins with a silent letter.

cake   flame   knot   autumn

(71)

GRAMMAR & USAGE

Write a plural noun in each blank.

two [foot] = _____

two [mouse] = _____

two [tooth] = _____

(72)

READING

Read the passage below.

   Leo studied all week for his spelling test. He practiced five words each night. On Friday, he spelled each word correctly on his test.

Write a title for the passage.

(73)

WRITING

Complete each sentence. Explain what these sentences have in common.

The Big Bad Wolf's teeth were as sharp as…

The Prince was as charming as…

Sleeping Beauty slept as soundly as…

(74)

PROOFREADING

Correct the sentence. Explain why you made each correction.

   Every month jasons grandmother sends him a new book in the male.

(75)

BONUS BUILDER #15

Complete the chart with words that are related to the city.

City Words		
adjectives	verbs	nouns

GRAMMAR & USAGE

WORD SKILLS

Add the same word to each word below. Write the four compound words you make.

set
down
shine
light

(76)

GRAMMAR & USAGE

Illustrate the subject in each sentence.

The car raced down the street.

The driver stopped at a red light.

(77)

READING

Circle the sentence that does not belong in a passage titled "What Roots Do for Plants."

Plant roots hold plants in the ground.

Roots get water for plants.

A carrot is a plant root that people can eat.

Plant roots absorb nutrients for the plant from the soil.

(78)

WRITING

Imagine that you just won $5,000. Write a statement, question, command, and an exclamation about your prize.

(79)

PROOFREADING

Correct the address.

king Fun E. riddle
12 funny bone ave
Laugh Lots, tx 78733

(80)

BONUS BUILDER #16

Write three goals that will help you become a better student. Explain how you plan to meet each goal.

WRITING

WORD SKILLS

Use the words in each group to form two contractions.

A.	B.	C.	D.
will could not	we will I	you have are	I am would

(81)

GRAMMAR & USAGE

Change the verb in the sentence. Rewrite the new sentence.

Pedro kicked the ball.

(82)

READING

Read the story.

Mark looked at the curtains that Bosco chewed. "If your dog doesn't behave, he'll have to go," Mom said. Without a word, Mark took the leash and carried his puppy outside.

Explain how Mark may feel.

(83)

WRITING

Complete the statement. Then write four sentences that support the statement.

_____ is the best _____.

(84)

PROOFREADING

Correct the sentences.

my dad werks at Tompson's printing company on eagle trail Drive. Mr. coder is her boss.

(85)

BONUS BUILDER #17

Spell five color words that have more than one syllable.

WORD SKILLS

WORD SKILLS

Write the word for each picture. Then pair the words to make three compound words.

86

GRAMMAR & USAGE

Make a list of five verbs that describe actions you might see at a soccer game.

87

READING

Number the directions from 1 to 4 to show the correct order. Tell what these directions are for.

- ☐ press the two pieces of bread together
- ☐ wash your hands
- ☐ get two slices of bread
- ☐ spread peanut butter on one slice and jelly on the other

88

WRITING

Make a list of ten things you need to do to plan a party.

89

PROOFREADING

Circle the letters that should be capitalized.

yesterday i went to see the movie *mars mania.*

90

BONUS BUILDER #18

Complete the key.

⊗ fair	△ school	⊠ make
Key = pre	= re	= un

WORD SKILLS

WORD SKILLS

List two words that have different endings and rhyme with *my*.

91

GRAMMAR & USAGE

Can you make all verbs past tense by adding *-ed* to the end? Explain your answer.

92

READING

Read the sentences.

Earthquakes can cause lots of damage. They can cause buildings to crumble, bridges to fall, and roads to buckle.

What does *they* refer to?

93

WRITING

Write a letter to your parents telling them about your day in school.

94

PROOFREADING

Add quotation marks to the sentences.

I think our field trip is tomorrow, said Mac.

It is tomorrow, said Michele.

Far out! replied Mac. I can't wait to go!

95

BONUS BUILDER #19

List two reasons why you might write someone a thank-you note.

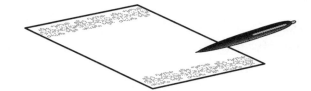

WRITING

WORD SKILLS

If the words below were on the same dictionary page, what might the guide words for the page be?

many	main	man
make	mall	mail

96

GRAMMAR & USAGE

Read the sentences. Complete the key.

Key
○ = there
○ = Their
○ = They're

● building a snowman.

⊘ snowman is on the hill.

Look up ⊕ to see the snowman.

97

READING

Read the TV schedule. List all the shows that are less than 60 minutes long.

Morning TV Schedule				
Channel	8:00	8:30	9:00	9:30	10:00
3	Weather 4U!		Cooking with Deb	Work Out!
5	Wildlife	Sports News		Cartoon Capers
7	Super Spy	Comedy Time	Space Voyage	

98

WRITING

Write about a time you had to be really brave.

99

PROOFREADING

Which sentence does not have any mistakes? Which sentence has the most mistakes?

A. I can't wait to go to the fare.
B. their are good rides and food at the fair
C. There are lots of fun games at the fair too!

100

BONUS BUILDER #20

Read the passage.

It's Sunday morning, and Tim and Tom are hiking in the woods. All the winter snow has melted. The trees are green and the flowers are starting to bloom.

What season is it?

READING

WORD SKILLS

Complete each problem.

do + not = _____

we + would = _____

he'll – will = _____

they're – are = _____

101

GRAMMAR & USAGE

Complete the chart. What is the rule for finding the output?

Input	Output
count	counted
see	saw
go	
shake	
sit	

102

READING

What do you think will happen next in the story?

Sal opened the door. The lights were off and everything was quiet. Suddenly, the lights came on and all of his friends yelled, "Surprise!"

103

WRITING

Imagine that you are a tiny ant. Describe what your day would be like.

104

PROOFREADING

Explain what is wrong with this sentence.

Please dont play in the garden said Mrs Jones

105

BONUS BUILDER #21

Write directions telling how to tie a shoelace.

WRITING

WORD SKILLS

Which prefix, *re* or *un,* can be used to create the most words below?

____write   ____able
____even   ____make
____clear   ____fair
____play   ____happy

 106

GRAMMAR & USAGE

Rewrite the sentence below using *I* as the subject.

David walks his dog, eats a snack, and does his homework after school.

 107

READING

Read the sentences.

Reptiles—such as snakes, lizards, and crocodiles—are cold-blooded animals. But mammals—such as cows, sheep, and dogs—are warm-blooded animals with fur.

Draw each kind of mammal mentioned.

 108

WRITING

Write directions that tell how to get to the office from your classroom.

109

PROOFREADING

Correct the passage.

Paul love to watch things fly. He looks for birds plains helicopters and hot air balloons all day long Pauls eyes are allways on the ski.

110

BONUS BUILDER #22

Write two words on each line to complete the poem about bubble gum.

Bubble Gum
Bubble gum is
Soft, sticky

_____ , _____ ,

_____ , _____ .

WRITING

WORD SKILLS

Spell each word correctly and fit each word into the puzzle.

pleese
agin
adress
thier

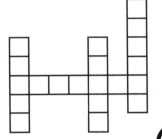

(111)

GRAMMAR & USAGE

Write three different adverbs that could complete this sentence.

Brad swims _____.

(112)

READING

Complete each sentence.

1. Zippers are to jackets as laces are to _____.
2. Earrings are to ears as necklaces are to_____.
3. Boots are to feet as hats are to _____.

Write a similar sentence of your own.

(113)

WRITING

Write a four-line poem about trees. Make the last words of the second and fourth lines rhyme.

(114)

PROOFREADING

Punctuate the sentence that needs quotation marks.

Thad's mom said that he could go outside after dinner.

Can I go outside tomorrow after dinner too asked Thad.

(115)

BONUS BUILDER #23

The parts of a friendly letter are the date, greeting, body, closing, and signature. Write a sentence to explain the purpose of each letter part.

WRITING

WORD SKILLS

Add *er* or *or* to each word. Then write a definition for each word.

teach   sail
lead   act

GRAMMAR & USAGE

Use the same predicate to complete each sentence.

The doors _____.

His eyes _____.

The stores _____.

READING

Read the passage.

Dan packed his model airplanes and his toys in the last box, and carried it out the door. "I am going to miss this house," he thought. "But the new neighborhood looks like fun, too."

Tell what Dan is doing.

WRITING

Describe what a person's face looks like when he or she is surprised.

119

PROOFREADING

List five things wrong with these sentences.

Michaels mom drived to phoenix, Arizona, last month. She went hiking swimming, and shopping there

120

BONUS BUILDER #24

List the words in ABC order.

cattle   campfire   chili
chow   coyote   cowpoke
corral

WORD SKILLS

WORD SKILLS

Use a contraction to complete each sentence.

_____ never seen a building that tall.

_____ see if we can ride the elevator to the top.

I bet _____ be able to see a lot from the rooftop.

(121)

GRAMMAR & USAGE

Match each subject to the correct verb. Use each matching pair in a sentence.

Subjects
dogs   she   we   dog

Verbs
talk   bark   talks   barks

READING

Which picture is not drawn according to the directions?

Directions:
- Draw a flower with four petals and two leaves.
- Draw two clouds above the flower.
- Draw a rock next to the flower.

(123)

WRITING

Add more description to the story by replacing the underlined words.

   Jason was so <u>happy</u> that he <u>jumped</u> two feet into the air. He <u>got</u> onto his new bicycle and <u>rode</u> off with <u>a big</u> smile on his face.

PROOFREADING

Correct the poem.

   one day in early may
   baby kay ran away
   not yet three years old
   baby kay is very bold

(125)

BONUS BUILDER #25

List five words that can be used in place of the water drop.

The swimmers into the water.

READING

WORD SKILLS

Write the same prefix to complete each word.

___ read   ___ do   ___ lock
___ pack   ___ tie   ___ used

(126)

GRAMMAR & USAGE

What can you do to turn each word below into an adverb?

quick   safe
sad   slow

(127)

READING

Read the passage.

    Pete ran like a cheetah around the track. He crossed the finish line ahead of all the runners.

Explain what the author means when he says, "Pete ran like a cheetah…."

(128)

WRITING

List the steps for brushing your teeth.

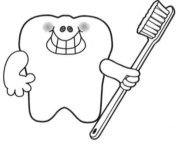

(129)

PROOFREADING

Correct the contractions.

    I dn't know why Shelly willn't write her name on her paper.

    I'l check and see why she keeps forgetting.

(130)

BONUS BUILDER #26

List each flight number in the order the flights arrived.

Evening Flight Schedule			
Arriving From	Flight Number	Scheduled Arrival Time	Remarks
Charlotte	841	5:48	one hour late
Detroit	250	6:29	on time
New York	453	7:30	on time

READING

WORD SKILLS

List ten five-letter words you can make using the letters in the word *strawberries.*

(131)

GRAMMAR & USAGE

Choose one of the words in each ( ) to complete each sentence. Explain each choice.

_____ bag is heavy.
(Al's, Als, Als')

The _____ are very nice.
(students', students)

(132)

READING

Write a title for the story.

Calvin woke up early on Saturday. He took his gardening tools and seedlings to the empty lot. He dug and planted all morning. Finally, the dirty lot had become a beautiful garden.

(133)

WRITING

Write a paragraph about bicycles.

(134)

PROOFREADING

Correct the passage.

Amy saw a zebra at the wilmington zoo. The zebras name was tiger. isent that a funny name for a zebra!

(135)

BONUS BUILDER #27

For each set of items, write a sentence to tell how the items are alike.

soap/sugar   tire/water
umbrella/watermelon   comb/smile

WRITING

WORD SKILLS

List three words that begin and end with the letter *d*.

(136)

GRAMMAR & USAGE

Use *good* or *well* to complete each sentence. Explain why you chose each answer.

That book is really_____ .
He reads really _____ .

(137)

READING

Would these sentences be found in a fiction or a nonfiction book? Explain your answer.

Greg and his family are getting packed for their vacation. They plan to spend two weeks on Mars visiting their relatives.

(138)

WRITING

Write a riddle that gives clues about your favorite animal.

(139)

PROOFREADING

Explain what is wrong with the sentence below. How can the sentence be corrected?

The first day of school was really fun on that day I met my new teacher and lots of new friends.

(140)

BONUS BUILDER #28

Write two sentences that belong in a nonfiction story. Write two sentences that belong in a fiction story.

WRITING

WORD SKILLS

The word *wind* can be pronounced with a long or short *i*. Each pronunciation has a different meaning. Write a sentence for each pronunciation. Think of another word that has two pronunciations and meanings.

141

GRAMMAR & USAGE

Write the real word for each made-up word below.

brang
knowed
catched
gooder

142

READING

What do you think will happen next in the story?

Francis rubbed the lamp until it shined. As he placed it on the table, he noticed a mist rising from its spout.

143

WRITING

What if one of your oars floated away while you were rowing a boat? Write about what you would do.

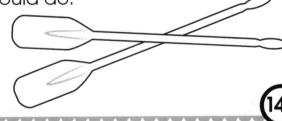

144

PROOFREADING

Correct the passage.

My family is going to fun world amusement park next weak. were gonna see shows and ride lots of rides. I can't weight to get there.

145

BONUS BUILDER #29

Study the proofreading marks. Complete the chart.

my dad makes ^the best Pizza (sp) I've ever tastd.

Marks	Meaning
	make a capital letter
(sp)	
	make a lowercase letter
^	

PROOFREADING

WORD SKILLS

The words *dad* and *mom* are *palindromes*—they can be read the same forward and backward. Write a palindrome for each clue.

1. the past tense of the verb do
2. the sound of a horn or whistle
3. the middle of the day

(146)

GRAMMAR & USAGE

Each bold-faced word in the sentences is a preposition. Explain what you think a preposition is.

Lisa has a mitt **in** her bag.

She went to play catch **with** her brother.

(147)

READING

Read each sentence about baseball. Underline each fact and circle each opinion.

Hitting a home run helps the team score.

Baseball is an exciting sport.

The pitcher throws the ball.

Batting is harder than pitching.

(148)

WRITING

Imagine you are a small baby. List five things you might be thinking about.

(149)

PROOFREADING

What type of mistake does the writer keep making in the sentences below?

Next year I am going to mexico. I want to learn to speak spanish before my trip.

(150)

BONUS BUILDER #30

Draw and label three other bees that could live in this hive.

WORD SKILLS

WORD SKILLS

Add a prefix and a suffix to change the meaning of each word.

_____ like _____

_____ use _____

_____ spell _____

(151)

GRAMMAR & USAGE

Rewrite the address. Use an abbreviation for each underlined word.

<u>Mister</u> and <u>Mistress</u> Frank Black
1234 <u>South</u> Andover <u>Avenue</u>
Brooklyn, <u>New York</u> 11205

(152)

READING

Write three false statements about the graph.

Favorite Animals

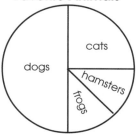

(153)

WRITING

Should students be required to wear uniforms to school? Write and explain your opinion.

(154)

PROOFREADING

Correct the letter.

Dear sue
    Can you come out and play
on friday. We could swing swim
and slide in my backyard.
          your friend
          kelly

(155)

BONUS BUILDER #31

If you were going antonym fishing, which fish would you catch?

big huge   sweet sour

hard soft   near close

WORD SKILLS

WORD SKILLS

Complete the chart.

Word	Synonym	Antonym
	glad	sad
small		large
		adult
many		

(156)

GRAMMAR & USAGE

Which word completes the sentences below—*then or than*?

I like to read more _____ watch TV.

Eat your dinner; _____ you can have dessert.

My hair is longer _____ my mom's hair.

(157)

READING

Read below.

"Okay, kids. You're playing well. Keep passing and talking. Work together and we can win."

Explain who is speaking and to whom he or she may be speaking.

(158)

WRITING

Would you rather hold a frog or a hamster? Write three reasons to support your answer.

(159)

PROOFREADING

How many mistakes are in this address?

Dr E. A. webber
211 manor dr
richmond va 41873

(160)

BONUS BUILDER #32

How many contractions can be made using the words below? List each contraction.

she	have	would	will
am	I	not	they

WORD SKILLS

WORD SKILLS

Illustrate the word that has the largest number of syllables.

tickets   crowd
players   court
cheering   winter
basketball   hoop

(161)

GRAMMAR & USAGE

Use a pronoun to complete each sentence.

[   ] went to the beach.

[   ] played soccer.

Look at [   ] skates.

(162)

READING

Follow the directions.

Draw a creature with three legs, four arms, and one head. On the head, draw two square eyes, a triangle nose, and a large mouth.

(163)

WRITING

If you were the mayor of a city, what you would do to make the city clean and safe?

(164)

PROOFREADING

Correct the sentences.

Betsys dog boo had ate puppys. They are the cutest dogs ive ever seen.

(165)

BONUS BUILDER #33

Read the cause. Write three effects.

The radio is too loud.

READING

WORD SKILLS

Write a one-syllable, two-syllable, and three-syllable word related to summer.

(166)

GRAMMAR & USAGE

Complete each sentence.

It's _____ .

Its _____ .

(167)

READING

Read each sentence. Draw one line under each cause and two lines under each effect.

Troy ate so much cake that he got a stomachache.

His mother told him to rest, so he went to bed early.

(168)

WRITING

What if your teacher were writing on the chalkboard and the chalk suddenly came to life? Write a story to tell what would happen.

(169)

PROOFREADING

Is the total number of mistakes in the sentence greater than or less than five?

"Billy, come here, called Grandma riley. I've brought a surprize for you

(170)

BONUS BUILDER #34

Color the adverbs in each box. What pattern do you see?

tomorrow	hat	silently	book
soon	ran	near	see
softly	house	away	disk

GRAMMAR & USAGE

©2001 The Education Center, Inc. • *Mind Builders* • Language Arts • TEC1605 • Key p. 48

WORD SKILLS

Write a suffix in the center of the flower that fits each word on the petals.

care
wonder
cheer
delight

171

GRAMMAR & USAGE

Use the price list to find the total value of all the words listed.

Price List	
nouns = 4¢	adjectives = 2¢
verbs = 5¢	adverbs = 3¢

dog	tiny	quickly
small	loudly	child
ran	bone	barked

172

READING

Explain what the sentence means.

It rained cats and dogs all night long.

173

WRITING

If you could invent one thing in the world, what would it be? Write a description of your invention and draw an illustration to match.

174

PROOFREADING

Correct the passage. There are eight mistakes.

how important is swimming to a shark if a shark stops swimming it sinks and stops breathing luckily sharks are great swimmers

175

BONUS BUILDER #35

Read the chart. List two ways the animals are alike and two ways they are different.

Australian Animals	active at night	eats plants	eats meat	lays eggs
wombat	X	X		
platypus	X		X	X

READING

WORD SKILLS

In a haiku poem, line 1 has five syllables, line 2 has seven syllables, and line 3 has five syllables. Complete the haiku below.

Line 1: Summertime is here!
Line 2: _____
Line 3: I love _____

GRAMMAR & USAGE

Write the name of your favorite book character. Then write a noun, adjective, verb, and adverb related to the character.

(177)

READING

Write one sentence to summarize the passage.

It was Becky's turn to play. She sat at the piano. She took a deep breath and began to play. The music flowed from her fingers. Everyone cheered when she was done.

(178)

WRITING

List five things that could cause someone to shiver.

PROOFREADING

Take the extra words out of each sentence without changing its meaning.

• I grabbed me a snack on my way out.
• I'll leave my book on this here table.
• Where does he live at?

(180)

BONUS BUILDER #36

Would the sentence below be found in a tall tale or a fairy tale? Explain your answer.

One time Shelly captured 100 wild bears in an hour.

READING

WORD SKILLS

List three words in which *y* makes the sound for *i*.

(181)

GRAMMAR & USAGE

Complete each sentence. Use the word *to, too,* or *two.*

Mark and Casey went _____ the aquarium.

Mark saw _____ dolphins swimming.

Casey saw them _____ .

(182)

READING

What is the definition of the italicized word?

Some people who live in the desert are *nomads.* They move from place to place in search of food and water.

(183)

WRITING

Write a simile to describe each egg.

(184)

PROOFREADING

Write three sentences about yourself. Use proofreaders' marks to correct your sentences.

(185)

BONUS BUILDER #37

What does the word *bears* mean in the sentence below?

The American flag bears 50 stars and 13 stripes.

READING

WORD SKILLS

Which word can not be abbreviated?

Street   Sunday
Doctor   Mister
May   November

186

GRAMMAR & USAGE

Switch the predicates in the sentences below. Rewrite each new sentence and draw a funny illustration to match.

The teacher wore a nice dress.
The elephant ate a ton of food.

187

READING

Read the passage.

Charlie opened one eye and then the other. He wasn't ready to wake up yet. So he curled up by the pillow, tucked his head under his tail, and purred quietly until he fell back asleep.

Explain who or what Charlie is. **188**

WRITING

What smells and colors make you think of spring?

189

PROOFREADING

What mistake does the writer make in each sentence?

The girls is playing in the park.

The dog are barking in the backyard.

190

BONUS BUILDER #38

Complete the checklist to write a poem.

☐ On line 1, write a noun.
☐ On line 2, write two adjectives about the noun.
☐ On line 3, write three verbs about the noun.
☐ On line 4, write two adverbs about the noun.
☐ On line 5, write a second noun that has the same meaning as the first noun.

GRAMMAR & USAGE

WORD SKILLS

Look at the problems below. Then write problems to show how to add *ing* to each of the following words: *name, run,* and *sniff.*

sigh + ing = sighing
hop + p + ing = hopping
solve - e + ing = solving

191

GRAMMAR & USAGE

Write three sentences about the beach that take place in the present tense.

192

READING

Explain how you know when you are reading a fairy tale.

193

WRITING

List five advantages and five disadvantages of being an only child.

194

PROOFREADING

Correct each title.

Topping it off!

How To Make A Great Pizza

a Slice of italy

195

BONUS BUILDER #39

Give an example of a time when you might have to read parts of an index.

READING

WORD SKILLS

Study the problems. What word does each symbol represent?

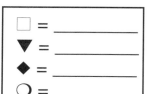

□ + ▼ = isn't
◆ + ○ = she'll
○ + ▼ = won't

□ = _____
▼ = _____
◆ = _____
○ = _____

(196)

GRAMMAR & USAGE

Write two sentences that include the word *run.* In one sentence use the word as a noun. In another sentence use the word as a verb.

(197)

READING

Write the title of your favorite book. List three facts and three opinions about the book.

(198)

WRITING

Describe how you think you will look when you become an adult. List some things that you want to do when you grow up.

(199)

PROOFREADING

Correct the passage.

   we enjoy a beautiful day at the park yesterday. We take a picnic lunch to eat under the beutiful summer sky and we also went on a nature hike through the woods and we can't wait to vist the park again.

(200)

BONUS BUILDER #40

For each item below, write adjectives that describe how the food looks, tastes, smells, feels, and sounds when eaten.

GRAMMAR & USAGE

WORD SKILLS

Answer each riddle with a pair of homophones.

What do you call…
a riding animal with a sore throat?

a bucket that has no color? rabbit's fur?

201

GRAMMAR & USAGE

Explain the difference between a common noun and a proper noun.

202

READING

When Patty's dad noticed that she was running late for school, he told Patty that she had better shake a leg. What did he mean?

203

WRITING

Make a list of five items related to a computer. Illustrate each item.

204

PROOFREADING

Biz E. Bee is mailing a letter to her friend. What is wrong with the way the envelope is addressed?

Butter Fly
123 Caterpillar Lane
Monarch, NJ 12345

USA 33¢
FREEDOM OF CONSCIENCE AN AMERICAN RIGHT

Biz E. Bee
321 Hive Road
Honey, AL 54321

205

BONUS BUILDER #41

Write a paragraph about how the world might be different if electricity didn't exist.

WRITING

WORD SKILLS

Use the key to find out how much the word *unlikable* is worth.

Key

vowels = 1   consonants = 2
prefixes = 3   suffixes = 4
syllables = 5

(206)

GRAMMAR & USAGE

Explain what is wrong with the sentences below.

The hungry children eight ate hot dogs.

You could here the siren all the way from hear.

They new that they were getting a knew teacher.

(207)

READING

What is the main idea of this diagram?

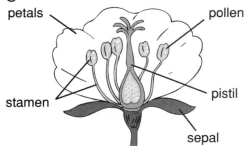

petals   pollen

stamen   pistil

sepal

(208)

WRITING

Write directions for riding a bicycle.

(209)

PROOFREADING

Explain what is wrong with the passage.

Logan enjoys soccer very much. She plays on a team at school. Ice cream is Logan's favorite dessert. Her soccer team is very good.

(210)

BONUS BUILDER #42

Write a word in each section of the diagram.

Short-Vowel Words   Six-Letter Words

Two-Syllable Words

WORD SKILLS

Answer Keys

Page 3

1. Students should have written the words *snake, whale,* and *sheep.* They should have also written two words to rhyme with each word. Rhyming words will vary.
2. Answers will vary.
3. *Ring* does not belong because it is not related to time.
4. Answers will vary.
5. soccer is my Favorite sport.
   Whats your favorite sport?

Bonus Builder #1: torn

Page 4

6. Answers will vary.
7. Answers will vary.
8. A. reads
   B. bat
   C. bus
9. Answers will vary.
10. mrs. tomie read to randy and carl on tuesday.

Bonus Builder #2: Can the baby walk across the room?

Page 5

11. Brian, Cindy, James, Kim, Lori
12. Plural nouns are nouns that name more than one person or thing. Students' examples will vary.
13. Possible answers include to a beach, to a water park, and to a pool.
14. Answers will vary.
15. The sentences contain six mistakes.
    Casey run as fast as she could to the finnish line?
    she won the Race.

Bonus Builder #3: The verb *walk* should be past tense.

Page 6

16. Answers will vary.
17. Fran likes tomato soup.
    The tree swayed in the breeze.
18.
19. Answers will vary.
20. close the door.
    bugs are Comming in the house.

Bonus Builder #4: *u*

Page 7

21. Answers will vary.
22. 2 frog   4 into
    6 pond   1 The
    5 the   3 leaped
23. movie theater, insects
24. Answers will vary.
25. Jake wint to play tennis with Luke after lunch on Saterday.

Bonus Builder #5: Answers will vary.

Page 8

26. baby, brown, bunk, and bush
27. an
28. no swimming allowed, railroad crossing, hiking allowed
29. Answers will vary.
30. Acceptable answers include
    Aunt Lily took Chase, David, and Sandy to the park.
    Aunt Lily took Chase, David and Sandy to the park.

Bonus Builder #6: Sarah's Favorite Movie is In The Days Of Dinosaurs. She Plans To Go See It With Her Aunt Rita Next Week.

Page 9

31. The word *dough* does not belong because *gh* does not make an *f* sound as in the other words. It also does not rhyme with the other words.
32. Is the apple on the table?
    Is the apple delicious?
33.
34. Answers will vary.
35. they right letters to each other once a month.
       (write)

Bonus Builder #7: a radio

Page 10

36. Picture labels: cookie, pizza, hamburger, and taco. Pizza and taco should be circled.
37. It's a chilly day.
    Please close the door.
    The cold air will come inside.
38. Do\you\like\ice\cream\and\cake?
    What\kind\of\ice\cream\is\your\favorite?
    What\kind\of\cake\is\your\favorite?
39. Answers will vary.
40. Jalen read the book to paula, Sam, and Tanya.
    They
    Them liked the story.
            (story)

Bonus Builder #8: Answers will vary.

Page 11

41. The following words are possible: brace, brick, clack, trace, track, and trick
42. Possible answer: I read a book while Tina watched a movie.
43. the airport; Students' explanations will vary.
44. Answers will vary.
45. The sentences contain five mistakes.
    come down from the tree.
    scared
    I am scary you will fall.

    Does you want to get hurt?

Bonus Builder #9: Answers will vary.

Page 12

46. isper   est   ase   ade   ame
47. Answers will vary.
48. Answers will vary.
49. Answers will vary.
50. less than three
    to
    it's too hot two sit in the car.

Bonus Builder #10: A cat

Page 13

51. Possible answers include *boot, loot, hook, good, toot, hood,* and *cook.*
52. Shelly buys a can of yellow paint.
    Shelly paints the kitchen yellow.
53. fiction, tall tales
54. Answers will vary.
55. Do you want a milk shake?
    I would like a chocolate milk shake.
    What a great tasting milk shake!

Bonus Builder #11: *Foot* and *great* do not fit because they do not sound like the other words.

Answer Keys

Page 14

56. *str*
57. book—add *s*
    leaf—drop *f* to *v*, add *es*
    dress—add *es*
    cherry—change *y* to *i*, add *es*
58. *Ice skating* does not belong. The other sports listed are team sports played with a ball.
59. Answers will vary.
60. rebecca found an ~~ear ring~~ (earring) on her way home.

Bonus Builder #12: Push the chare under the kichun tabel.
Correct spellings: chair, kitchen, table

Page 15

61. Answers will vary. 62. Answers will vary.
63. seven 64. Answers will vary.

65. Dear ada,
    I had a wonderful time at you're (your) aunt mary (Mary's) house. Shes a very
    nice lady.
    Thank you for a fun day.
                        Sincerely,
                        Leah

Bonus Builder #13:
[2] Drop a seed in the hole.
[1] Dig a hole in the dirt.
[4] Water the seed and watch it grow.
[3] Cover the seed with dirt.

Page 16

66. pets, step, pest 67. Answers will vary.
68. Answers will vary. 69. Answers will vary.
70. Answers will vary.
Bonus Builder #14:
                    are
hurricanes is large storms. They brings heavy wind and rain. they can
cause a lot of damage. People must be careful in hurricanes.

Page 17

71. silent letters—*e,e,k,* and *n;* unscrambled word—knee
72. feet, mice, teeth 73. Answers will vary.
74. Answers will vary. Each sentence contains a simile related to a fairy tale character.
75. Every month jasons grandmother sends him a new book
                mail
    in the (male).
Students' explanations will vary.

Bonus Builder #15: Answers will vary.

Page 18

76. sun—sunset, sundown, sunshine, sunlight
77. Students should have illustrated a car and a driver.
78. Plant roots hold plants in the ground.
    Roots get water for plants.
    (A carrot is a plant root that people can eat.)
    Plant roots absorb nutrients for the plant from the soil.
79. Answers will vary.
80. king Fun E. riddle
    12 funny bone ave.
    Laugh Lots, tx 78733

Bonus Builder #16: Answers will vary.

Page 19

81. A. couldn't, won't 82. Answers will vary.
    B. we'll, I'll
    C. you've, you're
    D. I'm, I'd
83. Answers will vary. 84. Answers will vary.
                                works
85. my dad (werks) at Tompson's printing company on eagle trail
                            his
    Drive. Mr. coder is (her) boss.

Bonus Builder #17: Answers will vary.

Page 20

86. foot, sun, ball, flower, house, dog; football, sunflower, and dog-house
87. Answers will vary.
88. [4] press the two pieces of bread together
    [1] wash your hands
    [2] get two slices of bread
    [3] spread peanut butter on one slice and jelly on the other
    The directions are for making a peanut butter and jelly sandwich.
89. Answers will vary.
90. (y)esterday (i) went to see the movie (m)ars (m)ania.
Bonus Builder #18: Key △ = pre ⊠ = re ⊗ = un

Page 21

91. Possible answers: pie, sigh
92. No. Students' explanations will vary.
93. earthquakes
94. Answers will vary.
95. "I think our field trip is tomorrow," said Mac.
    "It is tomorrow," said Michele.
    "Far out!" replied Mac. "I can't wait to go!"
Bonus Builder #19: Answers will vary.

Page 22

96. Answers will vary.
97.

98. Cooking with Deb, Work Out!, Wildlife, Cartoon Capers, Super Spy, and Comedy Time
99. Answers will vary.
100. The sentence with no mistakes is C. The sentence with the most mistakes is B.
Bonus Builder #20: spring

Page 23

101. do + not = __don't__
     we + would = __we'd__
     he'll – will = __he__
     they're – are = __they__
102. Rule: Form the past tense of each verb.

Input	Output
count	counted
see	saw
go	went
shake	shook
sit	sat

103. Answers will vary.
104. Answers will vary.
105. The punctuation is missing.
Bonus Builder #21: Answers will vary.

Answer Keys

Page 24

106. *un*

107. I walk my dog, eat a snack, and do my homework after school.

108. Students should have drawn a cow, a sheep, and a dog.

109. Answers will vary.

110. Paul (love) to watch things fly. He looks for birds (plains) helicopters, and hot air balloons all day long. Pauls eyes are (allways) on the (ski)
   loves *planes* *always* *sky*

Bonus Builder #22: Answers will vary.

Page 25

111.
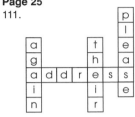

112. Answers will vary.

113. Zippers are to jackets as laces are to _____ shoes _____.
   Earrings are to ears as necklaces are to _____ necks _____.
   Boots are to feet as hats are to _____ heads _____.
   Students' sentences will vary.

114. Answers will vary.

115. "Can I go outside tomorrow after dinner too?" asked Thad.

Bonus Builder #23: The *date* tells when the letter was written.
   The *greeting* tells to whom the letter was written.
   The *body* tells what the letter is about.
   The *closing* brings the letter to an end.
   The *signature* tells who wrote the letter.

Page 26

116. teacher—one who teaches
   leader—one who leads
   sailor—one who sails
   actor—one who acts

117. Answers will vary.

118. Dan is moving to a new home.

119. Answers will vary.

120. 1. There should be an apostrophe before the *s* in *Micheals*.
   2. The past tense of drive is drove.
   3. The word *Phoenix* should be capitalized.
   4. There should be a comma after hiking.
   5. There should be a period at the end of the sentence.

Bonus Builder #24: campfire, cattle, chili, chow, corral, cowpoke, coyote

Page 27

121. Answers will vary.

122. dogs bark, she talks, we talk, dog barks; Students' sentences will vary.

123.

124. Possible answer: Jason was so <u>excited</u> that he <u>leaped</u> two feet into the air. He <u>hopped</u> onto his new bicycle and <u>sped</u> off with <u>an enormous</u> smile on his face.

125. one day in early may,

   baby kay ran away,

   not yet three years old,

   baby kay is very bold

Bonus Builder #25: Answers will vary.

Page 28

126. The prefixes *re* or *un* can be used to complete each word.

127. Add *ly* to the end of each word.

128. The author means that Pete ran extremely fast.

129. Answers will vary.

130. i (dn't) know why Shelly (willn't) write her name on her paper.
   don't *won't*
   (I'll) check and see why she keeps forgetting.
   I'll

Bonus Builder #26: 250, 841, 453

Page 29

131. Possible answers include *waist, waste, stare, stair, straw, sweet, sweat, swear, write, wrist, wiser, rarer,* and *erase*.

132. _____ Al's _____ bag is heavy.
   Explanation: *Al's* is used because the *'s* shows ownership.
   The _____ students _____ are very nice.
   Explanation: *students* is used because it's plural.

133. Answers will vary.   134. Answers will vary.

135. Amy saw a zebra at the zoo. The zebras name was tiger. (isnet)
   Wilmington *Isn't*
   that a funny name for a zebra?

Bonus Builder #27: Answers will vary.

Page 30

136. Possible answers include *did, deed, dad, dud,* and *dead*.

137. That book is really _____ good _____.
   Explanation: *good* is used as an adjective describing *book*.
   He reads really _____ well _____.
   Explanation: *well* is an adverb telling how he reads.

138. The sentences would be found in a fiction book because they do not describe realistic events.

139. Answers will vary.

140. The sentence is a run-on sentence. Students' explanations for correcting the sentence will vary.
   Possible correction: The first day of school was really fun. On that day I met my new teacher and lots of new friends.

Bonus Builder #28: Students should write two sentences that include realistic ideas and two that include imaginative ideas.

Page 31

141. Answers will vary.   143. Answers will vary.

142. knew, brought, caught, better   144. Answers will vary.

145. My family is going to fun world amusement park next (weak) were
   week
   (gonna) see shows and ride lots of rides. I can't (weight) to get there.
   going to *wait*

Bonus Builder #29:

Marks	Meaning
≡	make a capital letter
SP	fix spelling
/	make a lowercase letter
∧	add something

Page 32

146. 1. did   2. toot   3. noon

147. A *preposition* shows a relationship between a noun or pronoun and some other word in the sentence. Prepositions include words such as *on, above, in, across, below, to,* and *of*. Students' explanations of prepositions may vary.

148. <u>Hitting a home run helps the team score</u>.
   ⟨Baseball is an exciting sport.⟩
   <u>The pitcher throws the ball.</u>
   ⟨Batting is harder than pitching.⟩

149. Answers will vary.

150. The writer does not capitalize proper nouns.
   Next year I am going to mexico. I want to learn to speak spanish before my trip.

Bonus Builder #30: Answers will vary.

Page 33

151. Answers will vary.

152. Mr. and Mrs. Frank Black
   1234 S. Andover Ave.
   Brooklyn, NY 11205

153. Answers will vary.   154. Answers will vary.

155. Dear sue,
   Can you come out and play on friday? We could swing swim and slide in my backyard.

   your friend,
   kelly

Bonus Builder #31:

hard soft   sweet sour

Answer Keys

Page 34

156. Possible answers:

Word	Synonym	Antonym
happy	glad	sad
small	tiny	large
child	kid	adult
many	lots	few

157. I like to read more __than__ watch TV.
Eat your dinner; __then__ you can have dessert.
My hair is longer __than__ my mom's hair.

158. A coach is speaking to a team.   159. Answers will vary.

160. There are eight mistakes.

D & E. A. webber

211 manor dr.

richmond, vA 41873

Bonus Builder #32: 13—she'd, she'll, haven't, would've, wouldn't, won't, I'm, I've, I'd, I'll, they've, they'd, they'll

Page 35

161. Students should have drawn a basketball.
162. Answers will vary.
163. Students should have drawn a creature with three legs, four arms, and one head. On its head, the creature should have two square eyes, a triangle nose, and a large mouth.
164. Answers will vary.
165. Betsys dog boo had ate puppys. They are the cutest dogs ive ever seen. [eight puppies / I've]

Bonus Builder #33: Answers will vary.

Page 36

166. Answers will vary.   167. Answers will vary.
168. Troy ate so much cake that he got a stomachache.
His mother told him to rest, so he went to bed early.
169. Answers will vary.
170. greater than five
"Billy, come here," called Grandma riley. I've brought a surprize for you. [surprise]

Bonus Builder #34:

tomorrow	hat	silently	book
soon	ran	near	see
softly	house	away	disk

Page 37

171. *ful*   172. 32¢
173. It rained really hard all night long.   174. Answers will vary.
175. how important is swimming to a shark? if a shark stops swimming, it sinks and stops breathing. luckily, sharks are great swimmers.

Bonus Builder #35: Possible answers: The animals are alike because they can be found in Australia and they are active at night. The animals are different because they eat different kinds of food, and one lays eggs and the other one doesn't.

Page 38

176. Answers will vary.
177. Answers will vary.
178. Answers will vary.
179. Answers will vary.
180. • I grabbed me a snack on my way out.
• I'll leave my book on this here table.
• Where does he live at?

Bonus Builder #36: The sentence would most likely be found in a tall tale because it includes exaggeration.

Page 39

181. Answers will vary.
182. Mark and Casey went __to__ the aquarium.
Mark saw __two__ dolphins swimming.
Casey saw them __too__.
183. Nomads are people who move from place to place.
184. Answers will vary.
185. Answers will vary.

Bonus Builder #37: has or displays

Page 40

186. May
187. Students should have written and illustrated each of the following sentences:
The teacher ate a ton of food.
The elephant wore a nice dress.
188. Charlie is a cat.
189. Answers will vary.
190. The writer's sentences do not show subject/verb agreement.

Bonus Builder #38: Answers will vary.

Page 41

191. name – e + ing = naming
run + n + ing = running
sniff + ing = sniffing
192. Answers will vary.
193. Answers will vary. However, students should include fairy tale characteristics, such as magic, a happy ending, or patterns of three or seven.
194. Answers will vary.
195. Topping It Off!
How to Make a Great Pizza
A Slice of Italy

Bonus Builder #39: Answers will vary.

Page 42

196.

□ =	is
▼ =	not
◆ =	she
○ =	will

197. Answers will vary.
198. Answers will vary.
199. Answers will vary.

200. Possible answer: we enjoy a beautiful day at the park yesterday. We teake a picnic lunch to eat under the beutiful summer sky and we also went on a nature hike through the woods, and we can't wait to visit the park again. [enjoyed / took / beautiful]

Bonus Builder #40: Answers will vary.

Page 43

201. a hoarse horse, a pale pail, hare hair
202. A common noun names any person, place, or thing. A proper noun names a certain person, place, or thing and begins with a capital letter.
203. He meant that she had better hurry up.
204. Answers will vary. However, possible answers include monitor, keyboard, disk, hard drive, mouse, mouse pad, and CD-ROM.
205. Biz E. Bee's address should be the return address.

Bonus Builder #41: Answers will vary.

Page 44

206. Total = 41
Vowels (u, i, a, e) = 4
Consonants (n, l, k, b, l) = 10
Prefix (un) = 3
suffix (able) = 4
syllables (4 syllables) = 20
207. The pair of homophones in each sentence is used incorrectly.
208. parts of a flower   209. Answers will vary.
210. The sentence "Ice cream is Logan's favorite dessert" does not belong in the passage.

Bonus Builder #42: Answers will vary.